DOCTOR WHO
The Woman Who Lived

A story based on the original script by
CATHERINE TREGENNA

Level 3

Retold by Chris Rice

Series Editors: Andy Hopkins and Jocelyn Potter

Pearson Education Limited

KAO Two

KAO Park, Harlow,

Essex, CM17 9NA, England

and Associated Companies throughout the world.

ISBN: 978-1-292-20589-2

This edition first published by Pearson Education Ltd 2018

5 7 9 10 8 6 4

The authors have asserted their moral rights in accordance
with the Copyright Designs and Patents Act 1988

Set in 9pt/14pt Xenois Slab Pro

SWTC/04

For a complete list of the titles available in the Pearson English Readers series, visit
www.pearsonenglishreaders.com.
Alternatively, write to your local Pearson Education office or
to Pearson English Readers Marketing Department,
Pearson Education, KAO Two, KAO Park, Harlow, Essex, CM17 9NA

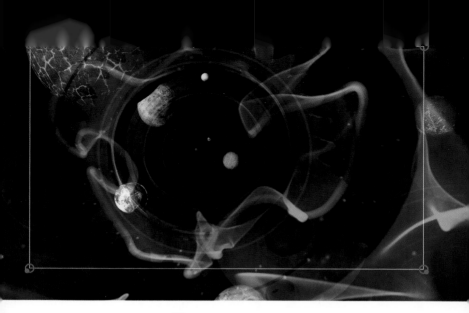

Contents

The Doctor and his Tools

The Doctor is an immortal Time Traveller from the planet Gallifrey. He travels through space and time, has many adventures and saves people in danger. Everyone calls him 'the Doctor'. He has two hearts and is about 2,000 years old. When the Doctor's body becomes old or ill, he changes it for a new one.

The Doctor doesn't use a gun, and tries not to kill anyone. But he does use special equipment which is not yet known to science on Earth.

His *curioscanner* is a hand-held machine that helps the Doctor to find hidden things of great importance or interest. His *sonic sunglasses* help the Doctor to see in the dark. They can also light fires. *Psychic paper* is a plain white card in a cardholder. The Doctor shows it when he needs to. The reader sees on it what the Doctor wants him or her to see.

An **immortality chip** is a small piece of soft metal that can bring a person back to life. It then makes them immortal.

The TARDIS

The Doctor travels through time and space in a time machine called the TARDIS. On the outside, the TARDIS looks like a blue police box from Earth. These boxes were used in the UK, many years ago, to call the police. The inside is a science-fiction spaceship, and is much bigger than on the outside.

The Doctor's Companion: Clara Oswald

The Doctor usually travels with someone from Earth. His companion is his assistant and friend, and helps him on his adventures. At the end of an adventure, the TARDIS returns the companion to Earth. They usually arrive back at exactly the same time as they left. In this story the Doctor's companion, Clara, is only seen in the last chapter.

Ashildr / Me

Ashildr is a young woman who was made immortal by the Doctor. 800 years after she and the Doctor last met, she has changed her name to 'Me'. She lives in a big house with her servant, Clayton.

Sam Swift the Quick

Sam Swift is a highwayman. He is dangerous, but can also be very amusing. People hate him for his crimes – and love him for his jokes and his enjoyment of life.

Leandro

Leandro is a Leonian; he comes from the star Delta Leonis. He is half-man, half-animal, with a head like a big cat. Fire comes from his mouth when he is angry. In 1651, he arrives on Earth.

Introduction

The highwayman climbed down from the black horse, took off the mask and walked slowly towards the Doctor. The Doctor couldn't believe his eyes.

'You!' he said quietly.

'Yes,' Ashildr said with a smile. 'It's me. What took you so long, old man?'

The Doctor last saw Ashildr in a Viking village, 800 years ago. When frightening visitors from another planet killed the village's best fighters, Ashildr wanted to fight back. With the Doctor's help, the Vikings finally won – but Ashildr died. The Doctor was interested in the young woman, and placed an immortality chip in her body. She returned to life, but became immortal and could never die.

At the beginning of this new story the year is 1651, Ashildr is a highwayman and the Doctor has just arrived on Earth again. How does Ashildr feel about meeting the Doctor after all this time? What does she think of being immortal? And can she and the Doctor still be friends – or will they become dangerous enemies?

The first *Doctor Who* story was shown on TV in 1963 in black and white. It was the first science-fiction programme for children in the UK and was very successful. More than 800 programmes later, the stories are funnier and more adult, but the central idea is the same. The Doctor travels through space and time in the TARDIS, his time machine, fighting dangerous beings from other planets.

Peter Capaldi plays the Twelfth Doctor. Capaldi has always loved *Doctor Who*. When he went into the TARDIS for the first time, he felt at home. 'I know how to work the TARDIS,' he said. 'I've known for a long time!'

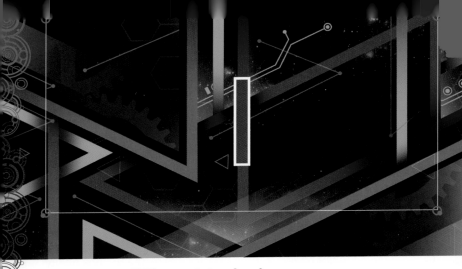

The Knightmare

It was night-time. Four white horses were pulling a carriage along a narrow road in a forest, the driver sitting between two bright lights. Suddenly, a masked figure on a black horse rode out of the darkness and stopped in front of them in the middle of the road. The carriage stopped and two very well-dressed passengers – one an angry-faced middle-aged man, the other a frightened young woman – looked out of the window. The masked figure rode towards them slowly and pointed a long, black pistol at them.

'Your money or your life,' said a deep voice from behind the mask.

'Do as he says,' the driver told his passengers nervously. 'I've heard of this highwayman. He's known as "the Knightmare"*. He's faster than Sam Swift the Quick ...'

'A stupid robber with an even more stupid name,' the Knightmare told the driver impatiently. 'Now,' he said, turning back to the passengers, 'I want your money, jewellery – everything.'

'One silly man on a black horse is not going to rob me!' said the angry passenger, looking ready for a fight.

*Knightmare: an amusing name for the highwayman. A nightmare is a bad dream. A knight was an important man, often seen on horseback.

'Who says I'm alone?' the Knightmare quietly replied.

Just then, two small, yellow lights shone from the darkness of the trees like the eyes of a dangerous wild animal.

The young woman in the carriage screamed.

In the middle of the same forest, the Doctor stepped out of the TARDIS and looked around, a serious look in his eyes. He held a small electronic machine in his hands. He switched it on. There was a soft ringing noise, and two red lights shone from its front. He studied the lights and listened to the noise carefully. They seemed to be giving him information.

'It's close,' he said quietly to himself. Keeping his eyes on the machine, he walked a few metres away from the TARDIS. 'Ah,' he said, looking more excited. 'Closer ...'

Then, with a small, mysterious smile, he followed the red lights into the trees.

The driver noticed the two yellow lights in the trees. 'We're dead!' he shouted, frozen with fear. 'The Knightmare is not alone!'

The man in the carriage, less brave now, quickly handed the highwayman a small bag of money.

'This isn't enough,' said the Knightmare impatiently.

'What more do you want?' the young woman asked.

'You know what I want. Give me the amulet.'

Suddenly, before anyone could speak, one of the carriage doors opened.

'Hello,' the Doctor smiled pleasantly, climbing in. 'Don't be afraid,' he added, pushing politely past the surprised-looking passengers. 'I'm only going to be a minute ...' The ringing noise from his machine became louder. 'Oh, *very* close,' he said excitedly, pushing his head out of the window next to the highwayman.

'What are you *doing*?' the Knightmare asked, very confused.

'What are you *doing?*' the Knightmare asked, very confused.

The Doctor looked up and saw a pistol pointing at his face.

'Don't worry about me,' he said, completely unafraid. 'I'm just passing through. Like fish in the night.' He opened the carriage door.

'This is a robbery,' the Knightmare said.

The Doctor stepped down in front of the Knightmare, talking to himself. 'We don't say *fish* in the night, do we? No. It's another word ...' He shut the carriage door behind him and looked up at the highwayman. '*Ships* in the night. That's right ...'

'This is *my* robbery,' the Knightmare repeated. 'Move away, or I'll kill you!'

The Doctor looked hard at the highwayman. He seemed to be noticing him for the first time. 'I'm sorry,' he said. 'Were you talking to *me*? Try again. I promise I'll listen this time.'

'Step away now if you want to live,' the Knightmare said, waving his pistol angrily.

'Do what he says,' the driver told the Doctor. 'He'll kill us all if you don't shut your mouth.'

But the Doctor wasn't listening. His machine was ringing more loudly. 'Sorry, sorry,' he said. 'I really was planning to listen that time, but I didn't. My machine is telling me something.'

With those words, his eyes on the machine, he followed the sound to the back of the carriage. The ringing became much louder and faster. The Doctor stopped. He lifted his eyes and saw a heavy-looking wooden box.

'Yes!' he said excitedly. 'I've found it!'

The masked figure joined him at the back of the carriage and pointed the pistol down at the Doctor's head.

The Doctor looked up. 'Oh, no. Wait a minute,' he said, suddenly understanding. 'This looks like a robbery.'

'I'm robbing these people,' the Knightmare repeated coldly. 'You are going to get out of my way.'

'I only want one small thing from this box,' the Doctor patiently explained.

But before the Knightmare could reply, there was a sudden noise. The Doctor and the Knightmare watched with surprise as the carriage drove away at top speed into the night.

'No, no, no!' the Doctor shouted, running after it. 'Come back!'

But it was too fast. He stopped and turned back.

'Look what you've done!' the Knightmare said angrily.

'No. Look what *you've* done!' the Doctor replied. 'You stupid man. Why don't you show me your face? What's wrong with it?'

'Nothing, Doctor.' The voice behind the mask suddenly changed from a man's voice to the voice of a young woman.

The highwayman climbed down from the black horse, took off the mask and walked slowly towards the Doctor. The Doctor couldn't believe his eyes.

'You!' he said quietly.

'Yes,' Ashildr said with a smile. 'It's me. What took you so long, old man?'

'Yes,' Ashildr said with a smile. 'It's me. What took you so long, old man?'

'Who's Ashildr?'

Putting the mask in her hat, Ashildr walked away.

'Old man?' the Doctor said, looking displeased.

'These days, most people die before the age of thirty-five,' Ashildr said. Then, turning with a half-smile towards the Doctor, she added, 'Everyone except you and me.'

'Didn't you hear immediately that it was me?' the Doctor asked.

'Of course. You don't forget the man who saved your life.'

She turned round and looked at him. There was a softness in her eyes. 'It's good to see you,' she said.

'Really?' the Doctor said. 'You pointed a pistol at my head!'

'The Knightmare must be frightening,' Ashildr said, using her deep voice.

'A very good voice,' said the Doctor. 'How do you do that?'

'Practice.'

'I saw you when you were helping sick people in Africa. I was so proud of you.'

'Proud of me? You weren't even there.'

'Yes, I was. You didn't see me – but I saw you.'

'And you just left me there.'

'You seemed fine.'

Ashildr shook her head and smiled. 'It's not important. You're here now. Let's go for a drink somewhere.'

'Oh, no, this isn't a visit to a friend,' the Doctor said. 'I've got a job to do. I'm looking for a very special jewel, an amulet.'

'Why? What's so special about it?'

'It doesn't belong here on planet Earth – not in 1651. If it falls into the wrong hands, the world will be in great danger. My machine is helping me to find it. It took me to the carriage that you were robbing ...'

But Ashildr was only half-listening. She looked hard at the Doctor. 'You mean you haven't come for me?' She turned away sadly.

'Oh, Ashildr, I'm sorry ...' the Doctor began.

But Ashildr turned back to face him. 'Who's Ashildr?' she asked.

'You are. That's your name. Ashildr. I knew your father too. Don't you remember?'

'Yes,' she said slowly. 'I think I remember the village.'

'You loved that village.'

'Maybe I did,' Ashildr replied, but the news seemed unimportant to her.

The Doctor looked at her seriously. 'Everyone in that village loved you.'

'Well, they're all dead now,' she said, smiling bravely. 'And here I am. Immortal, thanks to you.'

'Ashildr ...'

'That's not my name,' she said. 'I don't even remember that name.'

'So ...' the Doctor said, suddenly unsure of himself, his voice shaking. 'Wh ... wh ... what do you call yourself?'

'Me.'

'Yes, you,' said the Doctor, more confused than ever. 'There are no other people here.'

'No, you don't understand,' Ashildr replied. 'I call myself "Me". I thought of other names. But they all died with the people who knew me. "Me" is who I am now. I'm nobody's mother, daughter, wife. I'm alone. Just Me. But it's not important ...' she said, quickly changing the subject. 'I must go.' She pointed to her horse. 'Jump on. I'll give you a ride. You can help me.'

'With what?' the Doctor wanted to know.

'You'll see,' Me replied.

3

'800 Years of Adventure'

A full moon shone down on a large, dark, empty-looking house.

'It's a big place for someone who lives alone,' the Doctor said.

'I have a servant,' Me replied. 'And I have lots of visitors.'

As they walked towards the house, a large shadowy figure in the trees growled quietly. Me heard it, but she didn't seem surprised. She looked quickly at the trees and then followed the Doctor into the house.

Inside, Me walked past the Doctor towards a large wooden box at the foot of the stairs.

'What's the machine with the funny red lights that you were using?' she asked.

'My curioscanner,' the Doctor replied. He took it out of his coat pocket and switched it on. 'It helps me to find things from other planets. I've followed it for two weeks to here.'

Me opened the top of the large box and emptied her bag of stolen money and jewellery into it. 'Do you know what you're looking for?' she asked.

'I think so,' the Doctor said. 'Why do you ask?'

'I wasn't robbing the woman in the carriage – Lucie Fanshawe – for her money,' Me explained. 'She has often talked about having the strangest jewel in England – a very old amulet from a foreign country.' Me looked at the Doctor with a strange smile. 'Are we, perhaps, both looking for the same thing?'

The Doctor looked inside the large box. It was filled to the top with gold, silver, money and jewellery. 'You don't seem to need money,' he said, 'so why do you rob people?'

'For the adventure, Doctor.' She shut the large box and took off her coat. 'Isn't that what life's about?'

The Doctor followed her into a large library. Hundreds of books lined its walls. A fire was burning in a stone fireplace.

'I've had eight hundred years of adventure,' Me continued. 'Enough adventure to fill a library. And I've written it all down.'

The Doctor looked round at all the diaries, lost for words.

'Three hundred and fifty years ago I was a queen,' Me said.

'How exciting!' the Doctor said, his eyes lighting up.

Me gave him a bored smile. 'Not as exciting as you think,' she replied. 'It was all paperwork and card games. I escaped as fast as I could. I preferred being a soldier. Two hundred and thirty-six years ago I dressed as a man for the first time and fought against the French at Agincourt*. It was very exciting. Can you believe it? A woman helped to win the Hundred Years' War!'

'You're immortal,' the Doctor said softly. 'But you can still make mistakes if you're not careful.'

'It takes a thousand hours to learn a skill perfectly,' Me replied. 'After a hundred thousand hours, you're the best in history. And,' she looked at the Doctor proudly, 'I'm the best in the world at everything. At Agincourt, I was the fastest and strongest soldier on the field.'

'How many people have you killed?' the Doctor asked quietly.

'I don't know.' She looked around at the shelves of books. 'You'll need to check my diaries.'

'You can't remember?'

'If you're interested, I've saved a lot of lives too. Three hundred and three years ago I saved all the people in one village from a terrible sickness. But

---

*Agincourt: an important fight between France and England in 1415. The two countries fought many times in the Hundred Years' War (1337-1453).

'I dressed as a man for the first time and fought against the French at Agincourt.'

they weren't grateful. They couldn't understand how I did it. They were frightened of me. They thought that my great skills in medicine were a gift from hell. So they tried to kill me. They tied my hands and legs and threw me into a river. Luckily, I'm very strong – and I'm a wonderful swimmer.'

'The Black Death*,' the Doctor said thoughtfully. '1348. I was wrong not to tell you about that.'

Me looked at the Doctor, a tired look in her eyes. 'I got sick. But then I got better,' she said.

She sat down at a large desk and looked at the fire.

'Of course,' the Doctor said. 'Your body is learning to fight illness too.' He sat down opposite her. 'Another great sickness is coming soon,' he said urgently. 'And a big fire that will destroy half of London.'

This seemed to interest Me. 'Excellent,' she said, turning away from the fire. 'Maybe I'll start it?'

The Doctor shook his head. 'No. It will start by accident.'

'You really should read my diaries,' Me suggested again. 'I read them sometimes. Drink some wine. Let's have a little "Me" time.' She smiled, amused at her clever little joke.

'Why?' the Doctor asked, not amused. 'You don't seem to enjoy remembering things.'

'Exactly,' she said. 'I can't remember most of my past. That's the problem with immortality and ordinary memory. There's too much to remember.'

She looked sadly at the fire. The Doctor's eyes showed pity. 'It can't be easy,' he said softly, 'living longer than your loved ones.'

'It's hell,' Me quietly agreed.

They were silent. The Doctor looked down at his hands. 'I'm sorry,' he said.

Me looked at him with sudden interest. 'Tell me,' she said. 'What's it like to be sorry? I've forgotten. Feelings have come and gone. I never feel sorry, only bored. In fact, I've done all that I can here. I look up at the sky and imagine other planets, other worlds ...'

---

*The Black Death: a terrible illness that killed more than 75 million people in Europe between 1346 and 1353.

The Doctor stood up and started to walk away. Me watched him, and an urgent look crossed her face. She stood up too.

'Please, Doctor,' she said, following him across the room, 'take me with you. People here are only alive for a short time, then they disappear like smoke. You don't know what it's like.'

'I *do* know what it's like,' the Doctor corrected her.

'Then take me away with you in your time machine on your next journey,' Me said.

The Doctor turned around slowly. 'Tell me,' he said. 'How do you know that I have a time machine? You didn't see it when we met before.'

Me looked around the room for help. But she was a quick thinker. She looked the Doctor proudly in the eye and said, 'Because I'm unbelievably clever. But is it important?' Then, more softly, she repeated, 'Take me with you.'

'We'll talk about it later,' the Doctor replied.

Me picked up her coat from the back of a chair and put it on again. She looked at the Doctor with a friendly smile. 'The amulet that you're looking for ... I'll help you find it. It will be quicker.'

'I don't need your help.'

'Yes, you do,' she said. 'I know where Lucie Fanshawe lives. And I'm an excellent thief. We'll leave in an hour.'

With those words she walked out of the room, leaving the Doctor alone in the library.

4

'Me against the World'

The Doctor took a diary down from a shelf and began to read:

Today was the day that I died. But I was born again. A great man brought me back to life and made me immortal. His name was "the Doctor".

He smiled. Then he turned a few more pages and continued to read:

I had to leave the man that I loved. It broke my heart, but there were questions about me in the village. Years later, when I returned, he was dying of old age. But I still looked the same. He was confused. He thought I was a dream …

There were a few missing pages. 'Why did she pull these pages out?' the Doctor asked himself.

Then he found a page with very small grey circles on the paper. He studied them carefully. The circles looked like drops of water. And then he understood. 'The poor girl,' he said quietly to himself. 'When she wrote this, she was crying.'

He saw another diary on the shelf with the words 'The Black Death' on its cover. He opened it and began to read:

The children are holding toys as they sleep. I am on my knees in front of their little wooden beds. They will never wake up. My children. My screams. I could not save you, little ones. So much pain. But they are too young to die … I will continue to live this terrible, terrible existence. But no more babies. I cannot … will not suffer so much heartbreak again. In the future, it will be Me against the world…

The Doctor stopped reading and looked up. His eyes were filled with sadness.

While the Doctor was reading her diaries, Me was outside in her large garden. She was holding a candle in a small glass case and looking into the trees. A long, low animal noise greeted her from the shadows.

'Be quiet, my friend,' she said softly. 'We have a visitor. I didn't get it, but I will. If you keep your promise, I will have it before morning. My visitor will help me. Don't worry. He doesn't know about you. He only knows about the amulet. He has no idea what we plan to do with it.'

She smiled at the big, hairy figure in the darkness. Its two yellow eyes shone at her from its hidden face.

When Me returned, the Doctor was waiting for her outside the library.

'I read some of your diaries,' he said.

He waited for her to say something. She put out the candle and placed it on a table, but said nothing.

'Why are there some missing pages?' he asked.

'When the memories get too painful, I pull the pages out,' she said calmly.

The Doctor moved closer, giving her a long, disbelieving look. 'What can be worse than losing your children?' he said. 'Why didn't you pull *those* pages out?'

Me turned her back on him and walked towards the fire. 'I made myself a promise,' she said. 'Those pages help me to remember it.'

'What promise?'

'Not to have any more children.'

At first, the Doctor couldn't decide what to say. Then he said quietly,

'I've left you alone for too long. I didn't know how much you suffered. But I remember the person that you were. She's still there, inside you. I can help you to find her.'

Me put more wood on the fire. 'I don't need your pity,' she said coldly. 'I'm fine.'

The Doctor's face hardened. 'I think your coldness is just another mask,' he said. 'It protects you from the pain.'

She turned quickly to face him. 'I think you're frightened,' she replied.

He looked at her with great surprise. 'Frightened of what?' he asked.

'Of the person that I've become.'

'But this isn't a good way to live,' he said. 'You can't live a life without any feeling for the world.'

Me walked slowly towards him. 'So do you plan to repair me, Doctor?' she asked. 'Will you give me back my feelings and then run away again? No. I don't need your help, Doctor. You need *mine!* This time, you can't run away as you usually do.'

'How do you know what I usually do?' the Doctor replied. 'We met once, in a village 800 years ago. I didn't give you my life story!'

'But it's true, isn't it?' Me turned away calmly, picked a pistol up from the table and put it into her belt. 'You're the man who runs away.'

'Oh, and who told you that?' the Doctor wanted to know.

'Maybe I saw it myself,' she said. And with those words, she picked up her hat and mask and quickly walked past him. 'Let's go,' she said impatiently, leaving the room.

She walked outside, but the Doctor stopped at the door. He thought he heard a strange noise in the trees. He looked across the garden. Was there an animal or something watching from the shadows? He waited, then shook his head. 'Maybe I'm imagining things,' he thought.

Me was already a long way in front of him as the Doctor ran after her. He didn't see the yellow eyes watching him from the trees – or the ugly smile on the catlike face, with its lines of sharp white teeth.

The Amulet

A full moon shone down on Lucie Fanshawe's house as Me and the Doctor walked quietly towards its large front door.

'It's often difficult to break into large houses like this,' said Me.

'Not for me,' the Doctor replied. He reached into his coat pocket and pulled out some dark glasses. 'My sonic sunglasses can unlock anything.'

'Those won't be necessary,' Me told him. She pulled a piece of paper out of her pocket, opened it and showed it to the Doctor.

On it, there was a picture of a highwayman on a black horse.

Above the picture, in large black letters, were the words:

WANTED!
The highwayman known as
'THE KNIGHTMARE'

'Now is not the time to be proud of yourself,' the Doctor said.

Me said nothing. She pushed the paper under the door and pushed a very thin piece of metal into the lock. There was a soft noise as the key, on the other side of the door, fell out of the lock onto the piece of paper. She pulled the paper back from under the door, picked up the key and opened the front door.

'Now,' she said proudly, 'seems like a very good time to me.'

Then she took a black mask from her pocket and offered it to the Doctor. 'You'll need one of these,' she said.

'Thanks, but I already have one,' he replied. He put on his sonic sunglasses and followed Me into the house.

'It's as black as night in here,' she said quietly. 'I have a candle-lighter somewhere.'

The Doctor saw a candle on a small table. He looked at it and pressed a small switch on his sonic sunglasses. With a low, machine-like noise, they lit the candle.

'Very clever,' Me said without much excitement.

The Doctor began to walk away, looking very pleased with himself.

'Wait a minute, Doctor,' Me said. 'Do you know where you're going?'

The Doctor stopped, and Me took the candle from him.

'The servants' stairs,' she said. 'Follow me.'

Halfway up the stairs, the Doctor had a question for her:

'800 years ago I gave you *two* immortality chips. One brought you back to life. What did you do with the other one?'

'Not so loud,' Me said, turning to face him. She pulled something out from under her shirt and showed it to him. It was the second immortality chip. 'I keep it safely around my neck,' she said.

'But why are you still alone? Why haven't you used it – given it to someone special …?'

'Nobody is good enough to have one.'

As she continued up the stairs, the Doctor shook his head sadly.

'It isn't right …' he began.

But Me turned to him quickly. 'Be quiet,' she said, her finger to her mouth.

They watched from the top of the stairs as a door opened. A female servant came out of the room.

'Goodnight, Madam,' the servant said, looking back into the room.

The Doctor and Me waited nervously. Luckily, the servant didn't notice them. With a candle in her hand, she walked past them and disappeared round a corner.

'This way,' Me said, walking straight towards the door of the room next to the bedroom. 'That's Lucie Fanshawe's bedroom. So I'm sure that this is her dressing room.'

By the light of the candle, the Doctor saw that Me was right.

The room was filled with cupboards and wooden boxes. Me walked to the largest cupboard in the room and opened it. Inside were lots of smaller cupboards. She looked at them, confused. Suddenly, she heard a soft ringing noise behind her. She turned round quickly. The Doctor was walking towards her with the curioscanner in his hands. She was afraid that it was too noisy. She made an angry sign for him to switch it off.

But the Doctor walked straight past her and pointed the curioscanner at the smaller cupboards, one after the other. At one of the doors, the ringing noise became faster. He put the machine down, opened the door and took out a box. Inside the box was a shining purple amulet with two gold stones near the centre.

Silently, they both looked at the beautiful jewel. Then the Doctor spoke: 'The Eyes of Hell,' he said quietly.

Minutes later, they were downstairs. The amulet was safely inside Me's shoulder-bag. Then, as they were moving quietly towards the front door, a door behind them suddenly opened. It was another servant – a

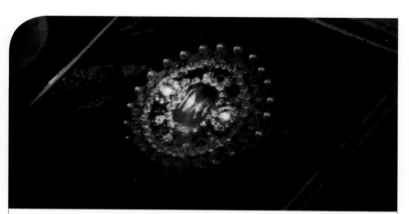

Silently, they both looked at the beautiful jewel. Then the Doctor spoke: 'The Eyes of Hell,' he said quietly.

man this time.

Me and the Doctor hurried into the nearest room and softly closed the double doors behind them. They looked around. The only light in the room came from five candles on a small wooden table behind a high-sided sofa. For a minute they waited. When they felt safe, they moved away from the doors, further into the room.

Suddenly, they stopped. They could hear the sound of a man talking. There, on the sofa, was Mr Fanshawe, Lucie's father. He was lying on his back, talking in his sleep.

Me put out her candle. The Doctor pointed past the sofa at another door on the far side of the room. They walked slowly, carefully, as quietly as cats, towards it. Halfway past the sofa, the wooden floor made a noise under their feet.

'Lucie?' her father called out loudly.

The Doctor and Me went down quickly on their hands and knees behind the sofa. They waited nervously as Mr Fanshawe moved sleepily away from them towards the double doors.

'Lucie?' he called again, more loudly this time.

Me looked over the back of the sofa, but the Doctor pulled her quickly back down.

'Lucie?' Mr Fanshawe asked, turning round. He was sure that someone was in the room.

The Doctor and Me froze as Mr Fanshawe, half-angry, half-confused, opened the double doors and stepped outside the room.

They got to their feet. The room was empty. Now they could escape. But the Doctor was careless. In his hurry to leave the room, he knocked over a metal tool in the empty stone fireplace. It made a very loud noise.

'There's a stranger in the house!' Mr Fanshawe shouted from just outside the room. 'Bring me my pistol!'

Me immediately took out *her* pistol and pointed it at the doors. She was ready for Mr Fanshawe!

The Doctor couldn't believe his eyes. 'What are you doing?' he asked angrily.

Me looked at him and replied calmly, 'If I don't kill him, he'll kill us.'

'No – we can't hurt him. We must hide!'

Me looked around the room. Maybe the Doctor was right. But where …?

Minutes later, the double doors flew open and Mr Fanshawe, pistol in hand, walked angrily back into the room. He looked around. It seemed empty.

'Guard the doors!' he shouted, as he walked past the empty fireplace. 'Call the soldiers!'

Luckily for the Doctor, Mr Fanshawe didn't notice the two black boots hanging down from the bottom of the chimney.

'Your feet, you stupid man!' Me said in a quiet but angry voice, pulling the Doctor up just in time. 'Oh, why did I listen to you? Why didn't I just shoot him? You're always making problems for me …'

Mr Fanshawe, pistol in hand, walked angrily back into the room.

'No,' the Doctor replied. He was as angry as she was. But he was careful to keep his voice low too. '*You're* the problem, not me.' He climbed up the chimney until he was face to face with her. There wasn't much space between them. 'I've had the same trouble with Clara,' he added.

Me suddenly forgot about the danger that they were both in. She wanted to know more about the Doctor's companion.

'So Clara's still with you, is she?' she asked.

'Oh,' the Doctor said, his nose almost touching hers. 'You remember Clara, do you?'

'Of course,' she replied. 'I'm always interested in other people's weaknesses.'

'Look everywhere!' Fanshawe's angry loud voice was dangerously near the fireplace. 'They will hang for this!'

The Doctor was worried. But Me was more interested in Clara.

'So,' she said quietly, 'what's wrong with Clara?'

'There's nothing wrong with her,' the Doctor said, climbing higher.

'Why didn't you make her immortal?'

'Well, look at you,' the Doctor replied. 'You're a fine example of an immortal.'

Me still didn't move. She looked up at the Doctor as he was climbing. 'She'll die one day,' she said. 'You know that, don't you? She'll disappear like smoke.'

'I already know that,' said the Doctor, losing interest in the conversation.

'How old are you, Doctor?'

'Older than you,' he said, still climbing.

But Me had one last question for him: 'How many companions have you lost? How many Claras?'

The Doctor suddenly stopped climbing. He seemed thoughtful. He opened his mouth to say something. But, at the last minute, he decided not to answer. He looked up the chimney with a serious look in his eyes and continued to climb.

A few minutes later, Me joined him on the roof. The full moon shone high above them, and the amulet was still safely in her bag.

Sam Swift the Quick

In the soft grey light of early morning, Me and the Doctor walked in silence along a forest pathway. Me was still wearing her hat and mask. While they were walking, they passed a gallows. There was no one hanging there that day.

'The hangman loves robbers, Ashildr,' said the Doctor, half-playful, half-serious. 'They keep him busy.'

'I'm not Ashildr,' Me replied with her usual seriousness. 'I'm Me. And I fear no hangman.'

Conversation continued like this for a short time. Then, suddenly, they heard a noise above their heads and a bearded man jumped from a tree onto the path in front of them.

'Sam Swift the Quick,' Me said calmly, almost bored. 'It's unwise of you to look so brave. Don't you know who I am?'

'The Knightmare,' Sam Swift smiled. 'And that's why I'm not alone.'

He was joined immediately by two rough-looking companions.

'Three against two?' Me said. 'This isn't a fair fight.'

'Was it fair when you started robbing people in my forest?' Sam replied.

Me quickly changed the subject. 'What's that funny thing on the end of your nose, Sam?' she asked.

Sam Swift touched his nose, looking confused. 'I can't feel anything,' he said.

'Oh, sorry. It's your face.' Me smiled childishly.

'Very funny.' Sam Swift laughed even more childishly. 'I didn't know you were so small and weak, Mr Shortmare!'

Sam's two companions thought that this was very funny. But Me was not amused.

'Perhaps I'm *small*,' she said. 'But I'm very *intelligent*.'

A dangerous look came into Sam's eyes. He took a pistol from his belt and pointed it at Me. 'Intelligence is useless when you're dead,' he said. 'Put down your pistol and give me your bag, or I'll shoot.'

The Doctor didn't want any trouble. 'We can give you some money,' he offered politely.

Sam gave him a long, hard look. 'Who's this?' he asked Me. 'Your assistant? You've got your Dad as your assistant?'

'I'm not his Dad,' the Doctor shouted, suddenly angry. 'I'm the *Doctor!*'

Sam thought this was very funny. 'The Doctor?' he laughed. 'Couldn't you think of a better name than that?'

'It's better than *your* name,' the Doctor replied quickly. 'Sam Swift the Quick? You look slow to me.'

Before Sam could reply, Me moved quickly. She took the pistol from his hand.

'You see?' she laughed. 'No one's faster than the Knightmare!'

But Sam wasn't as slow as she thought. He jumped at Me and fought her for his pistol. As they fought, the pistol fell to the ground. Me reached it first. Standing over Sam, she pointed the pistol down at his head.

Lying on his back, Sam looked up at the pistol. But he didn't look afraid. 'Put the pistol down,' he said calmly, 'or your assistant will die.'

Me looked over her shoulder. Sam's two companions were pointing their pistols straight at the Doctor's head. She put her pistol down. Sam picked it up and pointed it at the Doctor.

'Who's slow now, Doctor?' he smiled.

But the fight wasn't finished yet. With a quick movement of her leg, Me kicked Sam to the ground. Once again, Sam found himself on his back, looking up at his pistol.

His two companions looked away from the Doctor, their mouths open with surprise. This was a big mistake. The Doctor was too fast for them and, suddenly, their pistols were in his hands.

'Good question,' the Doctor replied, smiling down at Sam.

For the first time, there was fear in Sam's eyes. 'Please, Knightmare, I don't want to die,' he said.

Me looked at the Doctor. 'What do you think, *Dad?* Shall I kill him? He'll be dead soon even if I don't. Why not?'

The Doctor gave her a cold look. 'If you kill him, you'll make an enemy of me.'

Me lowered her pistol. She looked down at Sam and shouted, 'Run!'

Sam got nervously to his feet and ran away into the forest. He was closely followed by his two frightened companions.

The Doctor watched Me as she slowly picked up her pistol.

'I know their lives are short,' he said softly. 'But every life is important.'

'Be quiet!' she replied rudely. 'You're *not* my Dad.'

Without another word, she walked angrily away.

With a shake of his head, the Doctor threw the robbers' pistols into the trees and followed her slowly along the path.

'I know their lives are short,' he said softly. 'But every life is important.'

7

Leandro

At the foot of the stairs in Me's house, the Doctor called up: 'I have an idea about the amulet.'

Then he heard a cough. A door opened and an old, sick-looking man with long white hair walked slowly towards him.

'Good morning, sir,' the old man said weakly. 'Forgive me. Could you tell me who you are?'

'The Doctor.'

'I'm Clayton, sir.'

The Doctor smiled and then looked up. Me was coming down the stairs wearing a lovely red and white dress. Her long dark hair was piled up on her head. She looked beautiful.

'Would you like a drink, Lady Me?' Clayton asked.

'Yes, please.' Me smiled politely.

She waited with the Doctor while Clayton walked slowly and painfully back through the door. When the door closed behind him, they heard a lot of loud coughing.

'He can't see or hear much,' Me told the Doctor. 'He's completely useless. But …'

'But you can't send him away.' The Doctor finished the sentence for her.

'You see, you do have a heart. You're not as cold-hearted as you think.'

Me immediately changed the subject. 'How do I look?' she asked with a big smile.

'Red,' he replied. 'Are you ill?' Then, not waiting for an answer, he held up the amulet. 'Look,' he said. 'Why does an amulet from another planet look like the eyes of the King of Hell in old Greek stories?'

She took the amulet from him and walked quickly away with it into the dining-room.

Following her, he continued: 'In the Greek stories, the amulet protects dead people on their journey to a new life after death. Did that story, too, come from another planet?'

'I don't know,' she said, putting the amulet into her bag. '*You* tell *me*.' She looked at him. 'And you can't wait to discover *which* other planet, can you?' she said.

'No, no, you're wrong. I want to stay here with you for a short time ... '

'Why? To save me from a life of crime?'

'Why not? We make a good team.'

'Then take me with you,' she said quietly.

All excitement left the Doctor's face. He narrowed his eyes at her and said, 'You don't want to spend all your time with a silly old man like me. You have this wonderful planet to play with.'

'Why not?' she repeated more loudly.

'It takes a day here to travel fifty miles.'

'Don't worry. In the future, you'll be able to fly!'

'I want to fly *now!*'

The Doctor started to smile but changed his mind. Her unhappiness was real. She wasn't joking …

'I have waited longer than twenty ordinary lifetimes,' she continued. 'I've lost more than I can even remember …'

The Doctor said nothing. He seemed worried by her words.

'Please, Doctor,' Me said, almost crying. 'Get me out of this. I want more than this.'

The Doctor turned away, looking uncomfortable.

'Why not?' she asked.

The Doctor made no reply.

'Why not?' she repeated more loudly.

At last, the Doctor turned round to face her. 'Because,' he said, 'it's not a good idea.'

Something strange was happening to her face. It looked as hard as stone.

'Ashildr, please …,' he said quietly. He was unsure what she was thinking. 'Ashildr …'

'I am not Ashildr,' she replied, and her voice was as cold as ice.

There was a difficult silence between them.

Suddenly, there was a noise from behind the front door. It sounded like an animal.

The Doctor looked round quickly. 'Do you have a cat?' he asked.

Me didn't answer.

As the Doctor walked towards the door, the sound became louder. 'It sounds like a very *big* cat,' he said.

The sound of a faraway storm suddenly came nearer and the door flew open. There stood a large, handsome figure with long, gold-coloured hair and the face of a big, wild cat. He was wearing the skins of dead animals, and bright yellow lights shone from his eyes.

The Doctor backed away slowly as the figure walked into the room. Then he thought of Me. Her life was in danger … but no. The Doctor watched, confused. Me was completely unafraid. She walked slowly towards the

There stood a large, handsome figure with long, gold-coloured hair and the face of a big, wild cat.

catlike figure and stood calmly by his side.

'Doctor,' she said, amused by his confusion, 'I'd like you to meet Leandro.'

Leandro's eyes stopped shining. They became the eyes of a large cat – hungry, wild and dark with hidden danger – and they were looking straight at the Doctor.

'You thought that I was helping you,' Me said to the Doctor from Leandro's side. 'But the opposite was true. *You* were helping *me*.'

Without waiting for the Doctor's reply, she turned to Leandro.

'Leandro, we have it,' she said proudly. 'My friend here was very useful.'

'I don't understand,' the Doctor said. 'If you needed my help, why didn't you just ask?' He took a step towards Me. 'Or do you have secret plans that I won't like, Ashildr?'

'Stop calling me that,' she replied coldly.

The Doctor thought for a minute, then turned, suddenly brave, towards Leandro. 'Kill me!' he shouted into his face.

Leandro looked confused. 'Why?' he asked.

'If you're planning something terrible for this planet or its people, you must kill me first.'

'You're inviting death?' asked Leandro, still confused.

'No. I want you to attack me first. Then I won't have to worry.'

'About what?'

'You.'

Leandro showed his sharp white teeth and laughed. He clearly thought that the Doctor was crazy. And if he was crazy, he was unimportant. 'You are not of this world or part of my plans,' he said. 'I have no fight with you.'

'Then tell me why you're here. What do you plan to do? If you don't tell me, you must try to kill me. But you need to be very quick and very sure.'

'I am from the star Delta Leonis,' Leandro explained. 'But death came to my people. My world was destroyed. My wife was killed as we escaped ...'

'And you travelled by using the amulet?' the Doctor asked.

'I lost it when I crashed to Earth.'

'I found him in my garden,' Me said. 'He slept there while I looked for it. We need the amulet to open a gateway to other stars, other worlds,' she added, with a smile.

'Oh!' The Doctor looked at Me with playful surprise. 'What's your plan, Ashildr? Do you imagine yourself as Leandro's new queen? Do you like the idea of looking after him? Do you want a life of looking for lost jewels? Do you want to be his messenger while he sleeps?'

'Don't be stupid,' Me calmly replied. 'You're like every other man. I'm not looking for a husband. I'm looking for a horse.'

'A horse?'

'To get me out of town. I need help to leave Earth.' She studied the Doctor's face for a minute, then quietly added, 'You said no.'

'I don't believe it,' the Doctor said, pointing with a laugh at Leandro. 'Do you think his story's true? Is that what you think?'

'He understands the meaning of being alone,' Me replied quietly.

'I do too,' the Doctor replied.

Me narrowed her eyes angrily at him. 'So how could you do what you did – to me?'

The Doctor shook his head. 'You want to escape? Then why don't you just escape? I have no problem with that.'

'The amulet,' Me replied. She looked shyly at the floor.

'There must be a death.' Leandro spoke for her. 'It is the only way for the amulet to work.'

'Ah, of course ...' the Doctor said, understanding everything. 'Each death makes a small hole in reality. The amulet can widen the hole ...'

'There's so much death here already,' Me said. 'What's the problem with one more?'

'So ...' The Doctor shook his head again sadly and looked straight into her eyes. 'Who's going to die so you can escape?'

They heard the sound of coughing from outside the room. The Doctor narrowed his eyes at Me's sudden, mysterious smile.

'Clayton!' she called in a loud, clear voice.

'Coming, Lady Me,' the servant's weak voice answered from behind the door.

Playing with Fire

A disbelieving look crossed the Doctor's face. 'You can't kill him!' he said, looking urgently at Me. 'He loves you!'

'To the end, it seems,' she smiled coldly.

Leandro took a step towards the Doctor. 'Would you prefer to take the old man's place?' he said. And, with a terrible laugh, he showed his teeth and shot fire from his mouth.

'Not the Doctor!' Me shouted at Leandro. 'We agreed!'

Leandro shut his mouth with an unhappy growl.

'Oh, Ashildr.' The Doctor looked angrily at Me. 'What happened to you?'

'*You* did, Doctor,' she replied coldly. '*You* happened.'

Me took the Doctor into a small room and tied him to a chair. As she started to walk away, the Doctor called after her. 'I know you've suffered,' he said. 'Your children ...'

At the word 'children', Me stopped in the doorway. She turned slowly to face the Doctor. 'Death comes to everyone,' she said. 'Life is short. People are stupid and unimportant. They have children, die, repeat the same mistakes. It's boring. And I'm caught here. I can't escape.' She walked slowly towards the Doctor. 'I was left here by the one man who knows all about immortality. But he can't understand my pain.'

'I do now,' the Doctor replied quietly. 'But ...'

'You still won't take me with you,' she said. 'You travel freely through time and space. But I have to live through every year, every month, every day. Day follows day. Hour follows hour ... What happens to people after you've flown away? Do you ever think about that? I live in the world that you leave behind. Because you left me here!'

'So why is that my problem?' the Doctor asked calmly.

'You made me immortal!' she shouted at him.

'I saved your life,' he replied. 'But your heart has lost all feeling, all kindness for others, and I didn't plan that. I only wanted to save a very frightened young woman's life.'

'You didn't save my life, Doctor,' she replied. 'You made me a prisoner inside it. And now...' She turned and walked quickly towards the door. 'Now I've found someone who can free me from the prison. Someone who understands.'

And, with a terrible laugh, he showed his teeth and shot fire from his mouth.

'Listen!' the Doctor shouted urgently before she disappeared. 'I don't know what your stupid cat-faced friend's real plans are. But I know that he's dangerous! When you have your first fight with him, he'll bite your head off! I promise you.'

'Maybe *I'll* bite *his* head off,' she answered. 'Perhaps I'll enjoy that.'

She began to shut the door, but the Doctor refused to keep quiet. 'You're playing with fire!' he shouted. 'If you open that gateway ...'

'Yes, Doctor? I'm listening.'

'You have no idea what terrible things will come through it!'

'That, in my opinion, is a very good reason to do it.'

She smiled proudly, but the Doctor noticed fear and sadness in her eyes. 'You're not like this,' he said more softly.

'This is *exactly* what I'm like,' she shouted back at him. 'This is what you made of me!'

The Doctor stayed calm. He looked into her eyes for a long time, then quietly said, 'He'll kill you.'

'He'll have to be fast,' she smiled. And then her smile disappeared. She looked at the Doctor seriously and spoke coldly, without feeling, 'And perhaps, if he does, that won't be a bad thing.'

Again, she began to close the door on him. Then, suddenly, there was a loud knock on the dining-room doors behind her. She turned round quickly.

'Lady Me?' a voice called urgently.

Forgetting to shut the door behind her, Me took a few steps into the dining-room. At the same time, the Doctor began to move his chair towards the open door.

Before Me could reach the dining-room doors, they flew open. Two rough-looking soldiers ran in, one of them tall and dark, the other short and fat.

'Oh, Lady Me!' said the tall soldier, taking off his metal hat. 'I'm so glad you're safe! We've caught Sam Swift. He says that the Knightmare came here.'

'I haven't seen him,' Me replied calmly.

'Sam Swift is going to hang for his crimes today,' the fat soldier told her. 'At Tyburn*, at midday.'

'In half an hour?' Me said, looking at a big wooden clock.

The Doctor, with great interest, was watching everything through the half-open door.

'Did you hear that, Doctor?' Me looked back at him over her shoulder. 'A criminal is going to die. Excellent. Nothing wrong with that.' Then, turning back to the soldiers: 'I haven't seen the Knightmare. But this man behind me is his assistant, the Doctor. He was robbing my house so I tied him to that chair.'

The fat soldier took a pistol from his belt. The other one looked at the Doctor and pointed his finger at him.

'You will hang for this!' he said angrily.

'No, no, listen ...' the Doctor said nervously. 'I was trying to help ...'

'Be quiet!' the tall soldier shouted.

The fat one shot at the wall.

There was a surprised silence.

Me spoke first. 'He needn't hang,' she said to the tall soldier with a friendly smile. Then, more seriously, 'But keep him safely in a locked room.'

Another door opened and Clayton came in.

'Was that the door?' he asked. 'I heard a loud noise.'

He looked at the two soldiers. Then he saw the Doctor, tied to a chair. Clayton gave the Doctor an unfriendly look. 'I'm not surprised,' he said, shaking his head wisely. 'It's always the quiet ones who are the biggest problem.'

Me quickly picked up a few things from the dining-room table.

'Goodbye, Clayton,' she said with a businesslike smile. And then, to the Doctor, quietly over her shoulder: 'You see. I'm less heartless than you think.'

And with those words, she left the room.

*Tyburn: a small village west of London where criminals were hanged in front of a crowd of people.

'While You Laugh, I Live'

The Doctor looked worried as the short, fat soldier untied his hands.

'Do I look like a thief?' the Doctor asked. 'I'm not your enemy. I'm on your side ...'

The fat soldier looked up at the tall one. They smiled unpleasantly, but said nothing. They were having fun.

'I'm a secret policeman ...' the Doctor said, but suddenly stopped. He thought for a minute, unsure of his historical facts, and then continued, 'Or maybe you don't have policemen yet?'

'You've had too much to drink,' the tall soldier laughed.

The fat one lifted the Doctor roughly to his feet.

'I'm a famous soldier,' the Doctor tried again, looking more and more worried. 'Look.' With his free hand, he took his psychic paper from his coat pocket and showed it to the soldiers. 'This proves that I fought bravely for Oliver Cromwell* against the King.'

He watched hopefully as the tall soldier studied it closely.

*Oliver Cromwell: a man whose soldiers fought the soldiers of King Charles I. Charles I was killed (1649), and Cromwell became head of the English government (1653-1658).

*Newgate Prison: a famous prison in London. Criminals were kept there before they were hanged. It was shut in 1902.

But the other soldier wasn't interested and pulled him roughly across the room. 'Tell it to the chief at Newgate Prison',' he laughed.

The Doctor refused to keep quiet. 'You want to catch the Knightmare,' he said. 'I do too. I want to help you.'

'But you were robbing Lady Me,' the tall soldier said.

The Doctor went quiet. He was beginning to lose all hope.

Suddenly, there was the sound of horses from outside. A carriage was moving quickly past the window. On the driving seat was a small figure whose face was hidden inside a big red hood.

'Look!' the Doctor shouted excitedly. 'That's the Knightmare! He's driving to see the hanging at Tyburn. You have to free me. Or take me there!'

'Do you want to hang too?' the fat soldier asked, pulling him back from the window.

'Will you take me there if I say yes?'

'Of course we will,' the tall soldier said, looking pleased. 'We'll get £20 for catching you.'

The Doctor looked displeased. 'Is that all?'

'It's a lot of money to us,' said the fat soldier.

'Then I'll tell you a secret,' the Doctor said mysteriously. The two soldiers suddenly looked very interested. 'I know where Lady Me keeps all her money. Almost £30 ...'

'Why didn't you tell us this before?' the tall soldier replied.

Five minutes later, the Doctor was on a horse, alone, riding quickly along the road to Tyburn. He wanted to save Sam Swift before he was hanged.

A crowd of local villagers were standing around the gallows at Tyburn. They were shouting and enjoying themselves. At the back of the crowd, next to a stone wall just inside the big gate, there was a carriage with two black horses. A woman was climbing down from the driving seat. She stood outside the carriage, pulled back her hood and looked at the gallows. It was, of course, Me.

Standing on the gallows platform were two bearded men. One of them, a big strong man with cold blue eyes, was the hangman. The other was Sam Swift. He was drinking nervously from a bottle.

The crowd was becoming impatient. Angry voices began shouting, 'Hang him! Hang him!'

Sam Swift thought for a minute. He took another drink from his bottle and began to smile.

'All right, all right,' he called. 'Calm down!'

The crowd shouted at him even more loudly.

'You're a lovely crowd,' he shouted above the noise. 'Thank you all for coming.'

The crowd slowly went quiet. They wanted to hear his last words. But they were also confused by his playfulness. Why wasn't he more afraid? Why was he smiling?

Sam turned to the hangman standing next to him. 'I'm glad you're here, Mr Hangman,' he said with a friendly smile. 'These people here don't seem to like me. If you go, they'll kill me.'

A few people in the crowd laughed at his joke.

Pleased with his success, Sam laughed too. 'The hangman's new at this job,' he said more loudly. 'He's more nervous than I am!'

Sam was enjoying himself now. 'Oh, yes,' he said, looking around. 'I'm glad to see so many friendly faces.' He pointed down playfully at one woman in the crowd. 'You remember me very well, don't you?'

She shook her head and looked away shyly.

'And you?' He pointed at another woman. Her face went very red. 'So many lovely ladies here, and each one is a friend! I'd love to introduce you all, but I can't remember any of your names.'

The men in the crowd looked angrily at the women, but most of the women were laughing.

Then the church clock rang twelve o'clock. Sam began to look worried. Everyone went quiet. The men in the crowd started taking their hats off. But Sam quickly told a few more jokes. Some people still thought they were funny. Others in the crowd were becoming impatient.

At the back of the crowd, Leandro looked out of the carriage window. 'It's time,' he said quietly to Me. Me slowly walked away from the carriage.

'Hang him now!' she heard Leandro's voice shouting from the carriage behind her.

The strong, clear, frightening shout was heard by everyone in the crowd. They too began to shout: 'Hang him now! Hang him now!'

Sam looked nervously at the crowd. At the same time, Me was pushing her way towards the gallows.

'One more joke, Sam,' a voice called from the crowd.

Sam drank from the bottle and smiled. 'All right,' he said quietly. 'While you laugh, I live.' Then, in a loud voice: 'It was raining on the way to the gallows. The hangman said, "You're lucky, Sam. I've got to walk home through this!"'

There were a few laughs. Sam didn't notice the strange figure in a large black hood getting out of the carriage at the back of the crowd. But, out of the corner of his eye, he did notice the pretty young woman in the expensive-looking red and white clothes. She was climbing the steps to the gallows and then talking quietly to the hangman.

Sam turned round and saw a bag of money in her hand. 'What are you paying for, my beautiful lady?' he asked.

'I'm paying him to give you a quick, painless death.' Me smiled at him kindly. 'I don't want you to suffer.'

Sam turned to the crowd and asked, 'Who'll be the last person to kiss me?'

Some women in the crowd called, 'Me!'

Sam turned back to Me. 'I think they mean you, Lady Me.'

Me gave him a quick kiss and smiled. Sam studied her face thoughtfully. 'I know you from somewhere,' he said quietly.

Me turned away, still smiling. Sam turned to the crowd again. 'Now,' he said, with a sad smile on his face, 'I really don't want to die!'

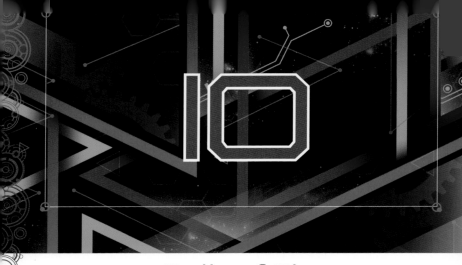

Balls of Fire

At last, the Doctor arrived at Tyburn. He left his horse outside the large stone gateway and ran past the guards towards the gallows.

'Excuse me, excuse me,' he repeated politely, pushing his way through the crowd.

Leandro, now in the middle of the crowd, turned and saw the Doctor. He looked back towards the gallows and, at the top of his voice, shouted, 'Time to hang!'

The hangman took Sam roughly by the arms.

'All right. All right,' Sam said, shaking him off. Then he spoke one last time to the crowd: 'Death is the biggest thief of all. It steals the most wonderful gift of all: life.'

The crowd went completely silent. Me looked first at the crowd, then at Sam. She seemed strangely nervous about something.

'The gift of a life filled with adventures,' Sam continued, smiling thoughtfully, but with a playful look in his eyes. 'And my life has had plenty of those.'

'I love you, Sam Swift!' a woman shouted from the crowd.

Sam was lifting his bottle for one final drink when, suddenly, he noticed the Doctor.

'Doctor!' he called. 'Doctor! Look at me. I'm a highwayman!'

He said nothing more. He looked hard at the Doctor, waiting for a reply.

Everybody in the crowd turned to the Doctor. He looked back at them, confused. And then he understood. Sam wanted him to make a funny reply. 'Er ...' He thought, at first not knowing what to say. Then an idea came to him. 'Keep taking the medicine!' he called back.

Everybody laughed. Sam looked pleased. 'Have you ever seen a Doctor so ugly?' he asked the crowd.

The Doctor didn't like that. He turned to the crowd and pointed at Sam. 'Have you ever seen a robber with a nose as big as that?' he shouted excitedly. 'It's so big ...'

'... that it can smell you from here!' Sam quickly finished his sentence for him.

The crowd laughed even more loudly. They loved this, and wanted more.

The Doctor smiled. He was beginning to enjoy himself too. Soon the jokes were coming quickly one after the other. But the hangman wasn't laughing. He looked impatiently at the church clock. The hanging was already five minutes late. He held Sam roughly by the shoulders and pulled him away from the crowd.

'Doctor!' Sam screamed. He wasn't joking now. 'I don't want to die. Help me!'

The Doctor thought for a minute, and then he had an idea. He pulled out his psychic paper and showed it to the hangman.

'I have a letter here from Oliver Cromwell. He says that you mustn't hang Sam Swift. He can go free.'

The hangman took the paper and studied the signature. Then he looked up at the crowd.

'It's true,' he said. 'This is signed by Oliver Cromwell. He says that Sam Swift is a free man.'

Sam fell to his knees and smiled gratefully up at the sky.

Some people in the crowd were happy, but others were less pleased. 'We've come a long way,' one man shouted. 'We want to see a hanging!'

'If not Sam Swift, why not the Doctor?' another man cried.

Many people in the crowd agreed. 'Yes, hang the Doctor!' they shouted excitedly.

A bright purple light shot up from the amulet and made a hole in the sky.

The Doctor, suddenly afraid, backed away from the crowd until he was pressed against the side of the gallows platform.

At the same time, Me tried to calm the blood-thirsty crowd. 'Do you want to see someone die?' she asked loudly. She took the amulet from a pocket in her dress and showed it to the crowd. 'Then watch this!'

'No!' the Doctor shouted at Me, climbing quickly up onto the gallows platform. But before he could stop her, she pushed the amulet hard against Sam Swift's chest. The amulet shone brighter and brighter. Sam, his eyes crazy with fear, became weaker and weaker. A bright purple light shot up from the amulet and made a hole in the sky.

'Purple – the colour of death,' the Doctor said quietly. 'It's taking away Sam's life and opening a gateway to other worlds.'

'To my new life!' Me added happily.

'Or to hell!' the Doctor replied.

Leandro, in the middle of the crowd, pulled back his hood and laughed loudly, fire shooting from his mouth.

The hole in the sky widened and a white planet came into view. Leandro jumped onto the platform next to Me and looked up at the sky with a hungry, excited look in his eyes.

'Goodbye, Doctor,' Me said with a cold smile.

Leandro looked down at her. 'You are going nowhere,' he growled.

'The gateway opens both ways,' the Doctor told her. 'You leave, but at the same time, the enemy comes in.'

For the first time, Me looked worried. Many small, bright lights started shining around the planet. 'What are they?' she asked, pointing up at the hole in the sky.

'Spaceships,' the Doctor said. 'They're coming through the gateway to attack our planet.'

Me turned angrily to Leandro. 'I thought that your people were dead,' she said. 'I thought that you were the last of the Leonians. That's what you told me. "You will escape from this terrible planet," you promised.'

'You *will* escape,' Leandro said, smiling unpleasantly. 'In death!'

There was a terrible crashing noise in the sky, and bright red balls of fire rained down from the enemy spaceships onto the crowd. Children were crying. People were screaming. Buildings started to burn. Soldiers shot up at the lights in the sky, but nothing could stop the fireballs.

'Doctor, what have I done?' Me turned to the Doctor, wide-eyed with fear. 'What have I done to these people?'

Leandro jumped down from the platform. He was crazy with excitement. A frightened man was running past him, and Leandro hit him to the ground.

'Stop it!' Me screamed down at him. She jumped down from the gallows and ran towards him. 'They can't defend themselves! Stop it!'

Leandro ran away and disappeared in thick black clouds of smoke. But she could still hear him laughing wildly.

The Doctor joined her on the ground as she looked for Leandro. 'Leandro feels no pity,' he shouted above the noise. 'He's not interested in the lives of others.'

'But I am!' Me replied.

The Doctor smiled at her. 'I'm glad to hear it!' he said. 'At last!'

Me looked at him, confused. 'We have to help them,' she said.

'Welcome back.' The Doctor smiled even more.

'Stop smiling and do something!' she screamed at him.

'OK,' the Doctor said, looking serious again. He walked back to the gallows, his face lined with thought.

Me followed him up onto the gallows platform. She stood next to him and waited patiently. Suddenly, he looked straight at her. 'Yes. We need to shut the gateway,' he said.

'I know that – but how?'

'Sam Swift. The amulet is still in him. When he died, the gateway opened. So what do we *do?*'

'We bring him back to life,' said Me.

'You cannot bring him back to life,' a voice growled from behind her. She looked round. It was Leandro.

'Oh yes we can,' Me said, completely unafraid. She reached inside her smoke-blackened dress and took the immortality chip from around her neck.

Leandro's face darkened. He tried to stop her, but he was too late. She pressed the chip against Sam's lifeless face. It immediately disappeared into his skin. Another strong purple light shone up from the amulet into the sky.

'No!' Leandro's voice was as loud as a storm. 'I was sent here from my planet to do a job. My people will destroy me for this!'

Sam's eyes slowly opened.

At the same time, the gateway in the sky began to shut. But before it shut completely, a bright light shot down from the sky. It crashed into Leandro. With one last, terrible scream, he disappeared forever in a cloud of silver smoke.

Sam sat up and looked around, confused. People nervously began to come from their hiding places out into the open air. The Doctor and Me both watched Sam carefully.

'I don't believe it,' Sam said. 'I'm alive!'

The crowd waved their arms and shouted with happiness. Even the hangman looked pleased.

Sam studied his hands and shook his head with a disbelieving laugh.

The Doctor looked at Me. Me looked at the Doctor.

'Welcome back, Ashildr,' the Doctor smiled.

'Are We Enemies Now?'

Some time later, inside a smoky pub, Ashildr, the Doctor and Sam Swift were having a drink together.

'I saw you in the crowd, Doctor,' Sam said. 'That's the last thing that I remember. I was very glad to see you. I didn't have many more jokes.' He looked around the table. He noticed that everybody's glass was almost empty. 'Let's have another drink,' he suggested.

On his way to the bar, he suddenly stopped. He turned round and looked at Ashildr. 'I haven't forgotten that kiss, you know,' he smiled.

When they were alone, Ashildr looked hard at the Doctor. 'Is he immortal now?' she asked.

'Do you want him to be?' the Doctor replied.

'I don't want *anyone* to be,' said Ashildr.

The Doctor noticed the serious look on Ashildr's face. 'Well ...' he began, looking uncomfortable. 'Probably not. The immortality chip worked very hard today. It brought Sam back to life. It also shut the gateway to outer space. Maybe it's too weak now to make him immortal.'

Ashildr shook her head, a look of both pity and amusement in her eyes. 'You really have no idea, do you?'

The Doctor looked away. 'No,' he agreed. Then, looking back at her, he smiled.

There was a short, friendly silence before Ashildr spoke again. 'You're still not going to take me with you, are you?'

At first, the Doctor didn't know what to say. He looked away thoughtfully. Ashildr waited patiently for his reply.

At last, he turned back to her. 'People like us live for too long,' he said softly. 'We forget the important things. Life is beautiful and special, but only because it's short. Sam Swift enjoyed every minute of his life. He even loved it when he was near to death. Now he's so glad to be alive. Look at him.'

Ashildr looked across the room. Sam was standing with the hangman. They were both laughing. She watched him in silence for a minute. Then she turned back to the Doctor.

'I looked into your eyes,' he said quietly. 'And I saw my worst fears – tiredness, emptiness ...' He looked at her with deep feeling, unable to finish his sentence.

Ashildr understood. She smiled sadly. 'And that's why you can't travel with me.'

'You're a very special woman, Ashildr,' the Doctor said. 'But ... I'll need to watch you carefully.'

Ashildr seemed pleased, but shook her head. 'No,' she said.

'No?' the Doctor said, surprised.

'Who is going to look after the people that you turn away from?' she asked. 'Someone has to. People need people like us. You'll be busy protecting the world. But it will be *my* job to protect the world from *you*.'

'So, are we enemies now?' the Doctor asked softly.

'Of course not,' Ashildr replied. 'Enemies are never a problem. But you have to be careful with your friends. And, my friend ...' She reached across the table and rested her hand on his. 'I'll be watching you.'

'Ashildr,' the Doctor said, looking at her warmly. 'I'm very glad that I saved you.'

'Oh, I think that everybody will be,' she smiled.

The Doctor narrowed his eyes, not exactly sure what she meant.

A Present for the Doctor

Inside the TARDIS, the Doctor was playing loud, electric music. He was deep in thought. The door opened and Clara came in.

The Doctor didn't notice her at first.

'Hello?' she said loudly.

The Doctor jumped. 'Oh, hello,' he smiled, switching off the music.

'Did you miss me?' she asked.

'Tell me who you are first.'

'Ha-ha,' she replied, taking something from her bag. 'I've got a present for you.'

'Why? Am I ill?'

'No.'

'Are *you* ill?'

'No.'

'Are you never going to travel with me again because I said something rude?'

Clara smiled but didn't answer. She walked towards him, looking down at an electronic camera in her hand. 'It's not a good present,' she added.

'I'm glad.'

She stood in front of him and looked up from her camera. 'OK,' she said, still smiling. 'Evie Hubbard.'

'Who?'

'Eleven years old? You helped her with her homework?'

The Doctor gave her a look. What was she talking about?

'She had to write an imaginary conversation with Winston Churchill*.'

'Oh, yes,' he finally remembered.

'Well ...' Clara said, looking down again at the camera. 'She got an A, so she's sent you a photo of herself.' She held the camera out. 'Look.' But the Doctor wasn't interested. He walked past Clara without looking. 'Yes, you're right,' he said. 'It's not a good present.'

'Look at it,' said Clara, following him with the camera.

'Why didn't you bring me some chocolate?' the Doctor continued. 'I like chocolate. Or even better – a fast car. A Ferrari perhaps?'

The Doctor, as usual, was acting like a child – a very rude and ungrateful child. But Clara knew that it was only his strange sense of fun. She stopped following him and turned away. 'Don't worry,' she said. 'It's not important ...'

The Doctor turned round immediately and started following her.

'All right,' he said. 'I was only joking. Show me. I want to see.'

Inside the TARDIS, the Doctor was playing loud, electric music.

*Winston Churchill: the head of the British government from 1940 to 1945 and again from 1951 to 1955.

Clara smiled. She turned and gave him the camera.

The Doctor looked at the photo and saw Evie standing next to Clara. They were both smiling, and Evie was holding her homework proudly up to the camera. But then he noticed something interesting. He moved his finger across the picture and made it bigger. Behind Clara's smiling face, watching from behind a large metal gate, was a small, smiling figure. It was Ashildr.

The Doctor studied the picture thoughtfully for a long time.

'What's wrong?' Clara wanted to know.

The Doctor looked up suddenly and gave her an unnaturally wide, toothy smile. 'Nothing,' he said, handing the camera back quickly.

Clara knew that he was hiding something. 'Doctor …?' she said.

But the Doctor didn't feel like explaining anything. He walked away and checked a few lights and switches in the TARDIS. 'In future,' he said over his shoulder, 'I'd prefer money, not presents. You can tell her that.'

Clara decided to change the subject. 'So,' she said, walking towards him, an excited look in her eyes, 'where are you going to take me?'

'Where do you want to go?'

'Somewhere exciting. Somewhere new.'

'There's nowhere new under the sun,' the Doctor said seriously. Then, with a sudden look of childlike excitement in his eyes, he added, 'But *over* the sun – that's different!'

His fingers danced lightly over some switches, feeding information into the TARDIS. At the same time, Clara threw her arms around him from behind and pressed the side of her face against his shoulder.

The Doctor looked up, quietly pleased. 'I've missed you, Clara Oswald,' he said softly, his hand resting on her arm.

'Don't worry, old man,' Clara said brightly. 'I'm not going anywhere.'

And with those words she moved away and stood in front of a large silver switch. She looked across at the Doctor.

'I'm ready when you are,' he smiled.

She pulled the switch towards her. Suddenly, the air was filled with the sound of the TARDIS as another journey through time and space began …

Activities

Chapters 1-2

Before you read

1 Read *In this story* and the Introduction at the front of this book. Then look at the pictures in the first two chapters. Discuss these questions with another student.

   a Who is the Doctor, and what does he do?
   b What is the date in this story?
   c When did the Doctor and Ashildr last meet?
   d How do you think life has changed for ordinary people between the time of their last meeting and the time of this story? Has it become easier or more difficult? Why?

2 Look at the Word List at the back of the book. Find words for

   a people
   b things that you will never find inside a house
   c things that you can wear

While you read

3 Are these sentences right (✔) or wrong (✗)?

   a Both passengers are afraid when they first see
      the Knightmare.
   b The passengers cannot see the Knightmare's face.
   c The Knightmare works alone.
   d The Doctor tries to save the passengers from the
      Knightmare.
   e The Doctor is unafraid of the Knightmare.
   f The Knightmare steals an amulet.
   g The Doctor is surprised to see Ashildr.
   h The Doctor and Ashildr last met in Africa.
   i The Doctor has come back to Earth to see Ashildr.
   j Ashildr has changed her name.

After you read

4 How are these things important in this part of the story?

a an amulet **b** an electronic machine **c** a wooden box

5 Discuss these questions with another student. Give reasons for your opinions.

a Is Ashildr pleased to see the Doctor?
b Is the Doctor pleased to see Ashildr?
c Has Ashildr really forgotten who she is?

Chapters 3-4

Before you read

6 How can the Doctor help Me, do you think?

While you read

7 Who is speaking – the Doctor (D) or Me (M)?

a 'It helps me to find things from other planets.'   .....
b 'I've written it all down.'   .....
c 'It was all paperwork and card games.'   .....
d 'They couldn't understand how I did it.'   .....
e 'It will start by accident.'   .....
f 'I do know what it's like.'   .....
g 'I'll help you find it.'   .....
h 'He has no idea what we plan to do with it.'   .....

After you read

8 Look at Activity 7, above. What does 'it' mean in each of these sentences?

9 Discuss these people's feelings. Why do or did they feel this way?

a The Doctor, when he sees Me's house

b Me, when she hears a noise from the trees in her garden

c Me, when she was a soldier

d Me, about her past

e Me, about her immortality

f The Doctor, when Me asks him to take her with him

g The Doctor, when he reads Me's diaries

h Me, when the Doctor offers to help her find happiness

10 Discuss these sentences with another student. Do you agree with them? Why (not)?

a Me isn't always honest with the Doctor.

b The Doctor likes Me.

c You can't live a life without any feeling for the world.

Chapters 5-6

Before you read

11 How will the amulet be important in the next part of the story? Discuss your ideas with another student.

While you read

12 Answer these questions about the Doctor (D) and Me (M): Who

a opens the door to Lucie Fanshawe's house? .....

b lights the candle? .....

c finds the amulet? .....

d makes a loud noise that Mr Fanshawe hears? .....

e is ready to shoot Mr Fanshawe? .....

f is careless when they are hiding from Mr Fanshawe? .....

g forgets that they are in danger? .....

h does Sam Swift think isn't very strong? .....

i fights Sam Swift? .....

j thinks everybody's life is important? .....

After you read

13 Correct these sentences about this part of the story.

    a Me shows the Doctor a piece of paper because she is proud of the picture on it.

    b The Doctor refuses to wear a mask because he already has one.

    c Me has lost the immortality chip that the Doctor gave her 800 years ago.

    d Me knows the way to Lucie Fanshawe's dressing room because she has been there before.

    e The Doctor opens a door, lights a candle and finds the amulet with his sonic sunglasses.

    f Lucie's father wakes up because the Doctor knocks over a piece of metal in the fireplace.

    g Me and the Doctor don't see Sam Swift at first because he is hiding behind an empty gallows.

    h The Doctor is amused when Sam Swift calls him Me's 'Dad'.

14 Work with another student. Have this conversation between Me and the Doctor.

    Student A: You are Me. You think it is better to shoot Lucie's father and Sam Swift. Tell the Doctor why.

    Student B: You are the Doctor. You think it is wrong to kill them. Tell Me why.

15 Discuss these questions with another student. What do you think?

    a Me says to the Doctor, 'You're always giving me problems.' Do you agree with her? Why (not)?

    b How does Me feel about the Doctor's companion, Clara? Why?

Chapters 7-8

Before you read

16 Look at the pictures in Chapter 7 and discuss these questions with another student.

    a Who is Leandro?

    b What problems will there be between Leandro, the Doctor and Me?

While you read

17 When do these happen to the Doctor? Number them 1-10.

a He tells Me not to use the amulet.
b He thinks that he hears a cat.
c Soldiers want him to hang.
d He thinks that Clayton's life is in danger.
e He hears news of Sam Swift.
f He is tied to a chair.
g He meets Me's servant.
h He meets Leandro.
i He knows that Clayton is safe.
j Me tells him why she needs the amulet.

After you read

18 Who is speaking? Who to? Why?

a 'He's completely useless.'
b 'It's not a good idea.'
c 'Do you have a cat?'
d 'There must be a death.'
e 'You can't kill him.'
f 'You're playing with fire!'
g 'That won't be a bad thing.'
h 'A criminal is going to die. Excellent.'
i 'You will hang for this!'
j 'I'm less heartless than you think.'

19 Are these people happy or unhappy at the end of Chapter 8? Why?

a The Doctor   **b** Me   **c** Leandro

20 Work with another student. Have this conversation about Me.

Student A: You feel sorry for Me. Say why.
Student B: You don't feel sorry for Me. Say why.

Chapter 9-10

Before you read

21 What are Leandro's real plans for the amulet and Me? Discuss your ideas with another student.

While you read

22 Underline the right words.

a The Doctor says that he fought *against* / *with* the king.
b The Doctor shows the soldiers his *sonic sunglasses* / *psychic paper*.
c The men in the crowd *like* / *don't like* Sam Swift's jokes about women.
d At 12 o'clock, Sam feels *less* / *more* hopeful.
e Me *wants* / *doesn't want* Sam Swift to feel pain.
f The Doctor uses his *sonic sunglasses* / *psychic paper* to stop the hanging.
g *Me* / *the Doctor* brings Sam back to life.
h Leandro *goes* / *doesn't go* back to Delta Leonis.

After you read

23 How are these important in this part of the story?
a jokes **b** money **c** the amulet **d** the psychic paper
e spaceships **f** the immortality chip

24 How do these words describe the following people in this part of the story? *the Doctor* *Me* *Leandro* *Sam Swift*
a confused **b** afraid **c** worried **d** happy **e** brave
f excited **g** kind

25 Work with another student. Have this conversation between the two soldiers.
Student A: You are the tall, dark soldier. You want to take the Doctor to Newgate Prison. Say why.
Student B: You are the short, fat soldier. You want the Doctor to go free. Say why.

Chapters 11-12

Before you read

26 Will the Doctor take Ashildr with him? Why (not)? Discuss your ideas with another student.

While you read

27 Tick (✔) the sentences that describe the Doctor and his actions.

a Sam Swift is friendly to him. ◇
b He doesn't know if Sam Swift is immortal. ◇
c He talks to the hangman. ◇
d He thinks that Ashildr will be happier without him. ◇
e Ashildr is still angry with him. ◇
f Ashildr doesn't want him to protect her. ◇
g He doesn't know who Clara is at first. ◇
h Evie Hubbard is grateful to him. ◇
i He doesn't tell Clara about his adventures. ◇

After you read

28 Work with another student. Have this conversation between the Doctor and Ashildr.

Student A: You are Ashildr. You still want to go with the Doctor. Tell the him why.
Student B: You are the Doctor. You still think Ashildr will be happier without you. Tell her why.

Writing

29 You are Me. What happened in the village 303 years ago (Chapter 3)? Write the complete story for your diary.

30 Would you like to be immortal? Why (not)? Give your reasons.

31 Imagine that Leandro is stopped on the street by some soldiers before this story begins. He is questioned by an officer. Write the conversation between Leandro and the officer. Begin like this: *Officer: Who are you and where do you come from?*

32 You are Lucie Fanshawe (Chapter 5). Write a crime report for the police after your amulet is stolen. How long have you had the amulet? Where did you get it? How exactly was it stolen? Who took it, do you think? How did the thieves escape so easily?

33 You are one of the soldiers who visit Lady Me's house (Chapters 8-9). Why did you go there? What happened when you arrived? How did the Doctor escape? Write your report.

34 You are Sam Swift. The soldiers have caught you and you are going to hang. You think that the punishment is too great. Write your speech for the judge. Explain why you should not die.

36 You are Me. Write an email to the Doctor after he leaves Earth. Describe what you are doing. Tell him how you are feeling. Ask the Doctor about his travels.

37 You are the Doctor. Imagine that you want a new companion. What kind of person are you looking for? What skills will they need? Write a letter to a Job Centre.

38 In Chapter 11, the Doctor says, 'Life is beautiful and special, but only because it's short.' Do you agree? Why (not)? Write 100–200 words.

Word List

amulet (n) a small piece of jewellery. Some people believe that it gives protection from danger.

candle (n) a thin stick that is burnt at one end for light.

carriage (n) a passenger vehicle that is pulled by a horse or horses.

chimney (n) the tall space above an indoor fire through which smoke escapes to the roof.

chip (n) a small, thin piece of metal or plastic carrying a large amount of computerised information.

confused (adj) unable to think or understand clearly. This is a feeling of **confusion**.

diary (n) a book in which you record the activities in your daily life.

figure (n) a bodily shape that can't be seen clearly. Perhaps it is too far away, or there isn't enough light.

gallows (n) joined wooden posts from which criminals were hanged. A gallows usually stood on a platform.

growl (n/v) a low, dangerous sound made by an animal.

hang (v) to kill someone by hanging them by the neck. Criminals were hanged by a **hangman**.

hell (n) in religion, the place where bad people go after death.

highwayman (n) a man, usually on horseback, who stopped travellers on the road. He pointed a gun at them and robbed them.

hood (n) a covering for the head and neck with an opening for the face, usually part of a coat or a jacket.

immortal (adj) living for ever.

jewel (n) a small, beautiful stone, often worn on rings or clothes at special parties. A lot of jewels are described together as **jewellery**.

mask (n/v) a covering for all or part of the face.

pistol (n) a handgun.

planet (n) a round body of rock and gas moving around a star. Earth, for example, is a planet that moves around the sun.

servant (n) someone who works in another person's house. He or she often lives in the house too.